anticipate

AN ADVENT EXPERIENCE

Paul Sheneman

BEACON HILL PRESS
OF KANSAS CITY

Copyright 2012 by Beacon Hill Press of Kansas City

ISBN: 978-0-8341-2857-6

Printed in the
United States of America

Cover: Lindsey McCormack

Interior Design: Lindsey McCormack

contents

7 | *Introduction*

10 | **Jesse Tree: Isaiah 11:1-10 – Introduction to Jesse Tree devotional** (Saturday)

13 | **Advent Week 1 – Theme: Anticipate the Promise**
- Jeremiah 33:14-16 – The Promise
  - 16 • **Sunday** – God – Creation – Genesis 1:26-2:4
  - 19 • **Monday** – Adam and Eve – Promise to Care – Genesis 3
  - 22 • **Tuesday** – Noah – Promise to Protect – Genesis 9:1-17
  - 25 • **Wednesday** – Abraham and Sarah – Promise of Blessing – Genesis 12:1-9 & 15:1-21
  - 28 • **Thursday** – Isaac – Promise Provided – Genesis 22:1-14
  - 31 • **Friday** – Jacob – Promise Affirmed – Genesis 28:10-22
  - 34 • **Saturday** – Joseph – Promise of Providence – Genesis 37:1-11

37 | **Advent Week 2 – Theme: Anticipate the King**
- Malachi 3:1-4 – Prepare the Way
  - 39 • **Sunday** – Judah – Family of Kings – Genesis 49:8-12
  - 42 • **Monday** – Moses – God is King – Exodus 14
  - 45 • **Tuesday** – Israel – Ten Commandments of the King – Exodus 20
  - 48 • **Wednesday** – Joshua – The King Gives them the Land – Joshua 6
  - 51 • **Thursday** – Ruth – The Kinsman Redeemer – Ruth 4
  - 54 • **Friday** – Samuel – A King is Chosen – 1 Samuel 3:1-21 & 8
  - 57 • **Saturday** – David – The Shepherd of God's People – 1 Samuel 16

60 | **Advent Week 3 – Theme: Anticipate the Prophecy**
- Zephaniah 3:14-20 – On that Day
  - 62 • **Sunday** – Solomon – Wisdom – 1 Kings 3:3-14
  - 65 • **Monday** – Elijah–Idol Worship – 1 Kings 17:1-16
  - 68 • **Tuesday** – Isaiah – Prophecy of the Servant – Isaiah 53

71 • **Wednesday** – Jeremiah – Prophecy of a New Covenant – Jeremiah 31:31-34

74 • **Thursday** – Habakkuk – Faithful Waiting – Habakkuk 3:16-19

77 • **Friday** – Nehemiah – The Return – Nehemiah 6:15-16; 8; 9

80 • **Saturday** – Zechariah and Elizabeth – Anticipation – Luke 1:57-80

83 | **Advent Week 4 – Theme: Anticipate the Coming**
• Micah 5:2-5a – O Little Town of Bethlehem

85 • **Sunday** – Mary – Hope (Lily) – Luke 1:26-38

88 • **Monday** – Birth of Jesus – Manger – Luke 2:1-20
[CHRISTMAS EVE]

91 • **Tuesday** – Jesus Christ – The LORD (Chi-Rho) – John 1:1-14
[CHRISTMAS DAY]

95 | *Appendix: Suggested Family Devotional Practice For Anticipate*

Introduction

Advent is a season of preparation. Everyone participates in preparing during Advent. Yet, not everyone prepares in the same way. The world prepares during Advent by consuming the latest and greatest gifts. They are preparing for a time of celebrating the goodness of God's creation without acknowledging God as King and Lord. However, the Christian is to prepare during Advent by waiting, praying, serving, and living as a witness to God's reign in this world. One way of preparation leads to a meaningless manger with no hope. The other way of preparing leads to a baby Messiah with the hope of His return as Lord.

Advent is a Latin word that literally means "coming" or "appearing." The word invokes the story of Jesus who came to our world as God's Christ or Messiah. The word also reminds us that Jesus told us, "My Father's house has many rooms; if that were not so, would I have told you that I am going there to prepare a place for you? And if I go and prepare a place for you, I will come back and take you to be with me that you also may be where I am" (John 14:2-3). Just as our Savior prepares a place for His followers, we prepare for His coming again. For Christians, Jesus told us to not be troubled by His return to God the Father. Instead, we are to continue being faithful to the way of life Jesus taught us. If we do this then the preparation during Advent is one characterized by anticipation for a cosmic celebration at the appearing of the Lord Jesus Christ.

The Christian preparation for Advent is characterized by anticipation when we take seriously God's mission revealed in Jesus Christ. As we retell and reflect on God's story during Advent, we become attentive to God's plan to redeem and restore the world. As the Scripture from Genesis to Revelation unfolds, we are invited to see how Jesus is the central character in God's rescue mission to earth. We take this seriously by examining our lives and depending on the Holy Spirit to pattern our lives after Jesus and transform our hearts into a single passion to love God and others. If our preparation during Advent leads us to change our lives for God's glory, then our anticipation for the appearing of Jesus Christ will follow.

Jesse Tree & Lectionary

This book incorporates two Christian practices for the Advent season. The first practice is the Jesse Tree. The Jesse Tree first appeared several centuries ago as artwork in the church. In stain glass windows, the depiction of a Jesse Tree was a way to show and teach the family tree of Jesus.

In recent time, the Jesse Tree has become a family devotional practice during the Advent season to learn God's story. The daily practice includes the hanging of an ornament that depicts a scene or symbol associated with the reading of a story from Scripture. The stories cover the various episodes of the Bible from creation to the birth of Jesus. The practice is a way for Christians to learn the story of God and learn the importance of Jesus within God's redemptive history.

The second Christian practice is the following of common lectionary passages on Sunday. This practice connects churches around the world together as they travel the road of Advent. There are devotional reflections on the Old Testament passages for the four Sundays of Advent in this book. These passages connect the retelling of God's story through the Jesse Tree with the prophecy of God's Messiah found in the lectionary passage.

An Advent Experience

This resource is only a guide. Lives get busy during this time of the year, and making life busier is not the goal of this resource. The devotionals, readings, and other materials are all designed to help you enter more deeply into specific faith practices so that you can grow in God's grace. So we are giving you permission upfront to use this resource in a way that fits your lifestyle. If you have time to do all the daily devotions and readings, that's great. But if not, that's okay too. We want you to use this as a means of God's grace for your family in a way that works best for your family. We want you and your family to be free to enter fully into the Advent experience. Take time to read the "Suggested Family Devotional Practice For Anticipate" located on page 95.

SATURDAY ✦ Anticipate the Promise

DAILY READING

A shoot will come up from the stump of Jesse; from his roots a Branch will bear fruit. The Spirit of the LORD will rest on him—the Spirit of wisdom and of understanding, the Spirit of counsel and of might, the Spirit of the knowledge and fear of the LORD—and he will delight in the fear of the LORD. (Isaiah 11:1-3)

FAMILY DEVOTIONAL • Hang the Jesse Tree Ornament – Isaiah 11:1-10

THE JESSE TREE

Isaiah prophesied of a shoot coming from the stump of Jesse. The prophecy sends us in two directions at the beginning of Advent. First these words from Isaiah take us back to the scene where God is sending Samuel to anoint David, the son of Jesse, as the king of Israel (1 Samuel 16:1-13). These words remind us that God has chosen a people who are to bless all nations (Genesis 12:1-6). We are to also to remember that God has chosen Jesse's family to lead the people of God (Genesis 49:8-12).

Isaiah's words also send us forward to affirm God's faithfulness. Jesus is the leader from Jesse's family tree, and of the tribe of Judah, who fulfilled all the promises of God to Israel. It is Jesus who shows the way of faithfulness, justice, and righteousness that God has called His chosen people to live. It is Jesus who has blessed all nations by calling all people to repent and receive the good news that the kingdom of God has come near.

You are invited to affirm God's faithfulness again this Advent season. The Jesse Tree is an invitation to return to the story of God to trace the salvation history found in those pages. By walking through the stories from creation to Jesus Christ, you are invited to track God's love story with humanity. It is another opportunity to share in the same hope, joy, fear, awe, and wonder of Israel as they lived in anticipation of God's promises.

FOR CHILDREN

The Jesse Tree is Jesus' family tree. We are going tell stories of Jesus' family along with pictures from the Bible. We are going to do this every day until Christmas so that we can learn about Jesus and His family.

- Today, I wonder how you feel about our family.

- How do you think Jesus felt about His family?

- Who do you think was a part of Jesus' family?

PRAYER

Come Branch of Jesse once again and bring to completion all of the promises of God for your waiting creation.

Advent Week 1 ✦

The Promise
A devotional reflection based on Jeremiah 33:14-16

LIFE ISN'T NORMAL.
One day I asked a group of teenagers to draw a scene or write a story of a perfect day. I imagined they would share pictures and tales of self-gratifying experiences. I was prepared to see images of them receiving extravagant gifts or praise from their peers. I expected to hear them announce hopes in a day were they cured cancer or received an international award.

After several minutes, I asked for a volunteer to share. Jane innocently raised her hand and stood up. Everyone turned to give her their attention and Jane turned her picture around to reveal the image of a tall guy and short girl holding hands.

Being a smart aleck, I asked, "Is your perfect day meeting your husband?" Everyone laughed in unison, except Jane.

Jane gently replied, "No. My perfect day is to meet my father."

Jane went on to tell us the story of never knowing her father. We heard a fragmented story of her mother and father's relationship that had more questions than answers. She talked about being raised by her grandmother and shared some of her relationship with her mother. Then she carried us to moments in her life where she saw a proud father holding the hand of his daughter. She affirmed the love her mother had for her but expressed the hope for a day when she could know the love of her father.

Silence consumed our group. No one knew what to say. It seemed like everyone, except Jane, shared my expectations for this exercise. No one was prepared to hear that something is deeply wrong with the world. It seemed like all of us, except Jane, knew the love of a father as normal. In that moment, we were shocked back into the reality that sin tragically makes our dreams of a perfect day merely a hope for normal.

THE PROMISE OF NORMAL

In the beginning, God created the world normal. More accurately, the Scripture uses the word good. The goodness of God's original design for creation is God's normal, and it was supposed to be common to our experience of life. In short, we were supposed to experience harmony in our relationship with God, self, others, and the world.

All of that has gone terribly wrong because we chose to break the harmony of relationships by denying God. By breaking the one rule we had, we rejected God as God, and sin, which is abnormal to God's creation, became common. We began to experience dissonance in our relationship with God, self, others, and the world.

The people of God in Jeremiah's day were keenly aware of the commonness of sin. It was a part of their government and religious lives. At the time, Jeremiah and the people of God had experienced a series of four evil kings who rejected God and led the people to put their trust in other nations for their protection. Likewise, the religious leaders rejected God and led the people to put their trust in idols as their ultimate hope. Thus sin was common in every part of their life.

In this context, Jeremiah announces, "The days are coming, declares the Lord, when I will fulfill the gracious promise I made to the house of Israel and to the house of Judah." In a way, God is promising a perfect day when His normal is common again. On that day, God will provide a leader from the family tree of Judah and more specifically from the branch of David. The leader will make acting just and right common again. God also promises to make Jerusalem, the center for the worship of God in those days, a safe place. Righteousness will become a common characteristic for those who worship God. In all of this, God is promising them a day when God is once again treated as God and the harmony of relationships is restored.

A LIFE OF PROMISE

This Advent season we begin with the promise of God to provide a righteous one who will come from the branch of David. Though we are tempted to jump to a celebration of how God has already fulfilled this promise, we should wait. We should stay in Jeremiah's prophecy and with the people of God in those days in order to hear the gift of God's promises.

The people of God didn't know when or how these promises would be fulfilled. They still had to endure political, religious, and economic uncertainty in their day. They had to face the reality that sin was still common to their daily life at the market, in the temple, and with their family. Jeremiah announces these promises to God's people under the oppression of sin as an invitation. They are an invitation to a life of promise.

We're invited this Advent season to hear the promises of God and to live as though God's perfect day is today. This is not a naive approach to life where we ignore the commonness of sin. This is a hope-filled engagement with life where we focus on the fact that our God is God of all and we can trust His promise to live just and righteous lives in the here and now. Therefore, our preparation for the celebration of Christ begins with the embrace of the life of promise God extends to us. It begins by embracing God's perfect day as merely the normal day God originally planned for everyone to experience. It begins with the full commitment to obey His leading. It begins with hoping in the day when we will be able to meet our Heavenly Father and "know him directly just as he knows us" (1 Corinthians 13:12b, *The Message*).

DAILY PSALM

Praise the LORD! Praise the LORD, my soul. He is the Maker of heaven and earth, the sea, and everything in them—he remains faithful for-ever. (Psalm 146:1, 6)

FAMILY DEVOTIONAL • Hang the Jesse Tree Ornament – Genesis 1:26-2:4

CREATION

God said, "Let's make humans in our own image. They'll be responsible to take care of all we created." And God did just that.

Humans, male and female, were a part of God's plan for creation. All of us were given a unique role among all the creatures that God created. Our role was to represent God to all creation. Our passage talks about that role as being created in the image of God. In other words, we were created to reflect God's character and action in how we lived.

Being a representative of God to all creation was imagined to be like the role of the priest in ancient times. The role of the priest is to extend God's care and blessing to all people. They are to lead people to follow God faithfully. This is similar to the role God had in mind for all humans. We were supposed to reflect God's care and blessing for all in our actions and words. All humans were intended to faithfully follow God and so care for each other and all creation. In short, all of us are to be priests in God's grand temple, creation.

Jesus, the second Adam and great High Priest, is the fulfillment of humanities' role. Jesus reflects God's care and blessing for all and shows what it means to be a priest. By healing the sick, feeding the hungry, freeing those enslaved by demons, and forgiving sins, Jesus shows us what it means to be human as God intended from the beginning.

FOR CHILDREN

In the beginning, there was nothing. Then God said, "Let there be light." And there was light. Then God put water in the sea and clouds in the sky. Next He made land. After that He put the sun, moon and stars in place. He filled the sea and sky. Then He filled the land with all kinds of animals and made humans like you and me. This was the beginning of Jesus' family. Finally, God looked at all He made and said, "This is good!" So He stopped creating, rested and enjoyed everything He made.

• What do you like to do outside?

• How are we different from other things God created?

• I wonder how God wants us to care for His creation.

PRAYER

God of creation may you lead us in the way of Jesus to care for your creation and bless others in your name as witnesses of your Advent.

MONDAY ✦ Anticipate the Promise

DAILY PSALM

Blessed is the one who does not walk in step with the wicked or stand in the way that sinners take or sit in the company of mockers, but whose delight is in the law of the LORD, and who meditates on his law day and night. (Psalm 1:1-2)

FAMILY DEVOTIONAL • Hang the Jesse Tree Ornament – Genesis 3

PROMISE TO CARE

The original humans, Adam and Eve, were created to be God's representatives. However, they believed that they could live another way. They believed the lie that they might actually be able to be equal with God instead of serving their Creator.

They committed the original sin of pride by breaking the only rule that God gave them to follow. In doing this they destroyed human relationship with God, others and all creation.

At the end of this tragic story, God acts on behalf of the disobedient humans (Genesis 3:21-24). First, God makes clothes for Adam and Eve in order that they could cover their shame. Second, God makes sure that humans wouldn't have to live forever in their sinful way by guarding them from getting to the Tree of Life. In these two actions, we are given the promise that God is determined to care for sinful and disobedient humans and will ultimately deal with their guilt and evil way.

This Advent season we can anticipate the care of God for His broken humans and creation. In Christ's life, death and resurrection, God has set a termination date on our shame and the enemy of God, death. When Jesus Christ returns, God will judge sin and His care for all creation will be fully revealed.

FOR CHILDREN

Adam and Eve lived in a beautiful garden called Eden. God said to them, "Enjoy the garden but don't eat fruit from the tree of knowledge of good and evil."

One day a snake came up to Eve and said, "Why don't you eat that fruit?"

Eve said, "God told us not to or we would die." But Eve ate the fruit and Adam did too.

They both felt sad and tried to hide from God. God found them and made them leave the beautiful garden because they didn't obey His rule.

• I wonder how you feel when you don't obey the rules.

• I wonder how Adam and Eve felt when they didn't obey God's rule.

• I wonder how God felt when Adam and Eve didn't obey His rule.

PRAYER

Father, come to us in this time and care for our broken hearts. Forgive us of the brokenness that we spread and allow us to mend the brokenness in the world as we prepare to receive your Son again. Amen.

TUESDAY ✦ Anticipate the Promise

DAILY PSALM

Listen to my words, LORD, consider my lament. Hear my cry for help, my King and my God, for to you I pray. In the morning, LORD, you hear my voice; in the morning I lay my requests before you and wait expectantly. (Psalm 5:1-3)

FAMILY DEVOTIONAL • Hang the Jesse Tree Ornament – Genesis 9:1-17

PROMISE TO PROTECT

After a great flood on the earth, God creates a covenant, or promise, with Noah and all creation. The promise is to protect all creation despite the wickedness of humans. The symbol of God's promise is a rainbow. God promises to protect the world by never allowing the earth as a whole to experience the destruction of flood waters again.

God calls or invites Noah and his family to begin again with God's original plan for humans. In the language of Genesis 1:26-30, God charges them to be fruitful and multiply. In God's call to Noah, humans are given another chance to represent God to creation and to each other. God knows "every inclination of the human heart is evil from childhood" (Genesis 8:21), yet God loves and provides another opportunity for humanity to be faithful.

At the end of the story of Noah, the fulfillment of the promise already begins (Genesis 10). The seventy nations, which divided the Hebrew people from humanity are described as the descendants of Noah. Throughout God's story they will be referred to as the Gentiles or heathens and are the ultimate recipients of God's blessings. They are introduced here as a result of God's promise.

Jesus comes from the descendants of Shem (Luke 3:36) and is the fulfillment of God's promise to protect. Those who are in Christ are a new creation and the evil inclinations of the human heart are reoriented toward a loving God. Thus, Jesus provides the means for all humans, both Jew and Gentile, to be the source of God's protection for the whole earth.

FOR CHILDREN

Adam and Eve had children. Then their children had children, too. Soon there were many people on the earth. But they were unkind and bad.

God was sad because all the people were bad. He said, "I'll send a flood to wash my world clean again."

Then He noticed one good man. His name was Noah. God said to Noah, "Build an ark (a big boat) because a flood is coming."

But Noah kept building. When he had finished, God said, "Put two of every kind of animal in the ark."

Noah did what God asked him to do. And when all the animals and his family were in the ark, he shut the door. Then the rain came down for days and soon the ark was floating on the water. But Noah, his family, and all the animals were safe inside the ark.

One day the ark came to rest on land. Noah, his family, and all of the animals came out of the boat. And God put a rainbow in the sky as a promise to never flood the whole earth again.

- I wonder why God was sad that all the people were bad.

- How do you feel when you see a rainbow?

PRAYER

God of mercy turn the evil inclinations of the human heart toward your justice and love that we may know the freedom to love you as we are loved. Amen.

WEDNESDAY ✦ Anticipate the Promise

DAILY PSALM

I seek you with all my heart; do not let me stray from your commands.
I have hidden your word in my heart that I might not sin against you.
Praise be to you, LORD; teach me your decrees. (Psalm 119:10-12)

FAMILY DEVOTIONAL • Hang the Jesse Tree Ornament – Genesis 12:1-9 & 15:1-21

PROMISE OF BLESSING

Abraham and Sarah begin a completely new journey for humans. Abraham is a wealthy man living in a safe city with his family when God calls him to travel to an unknown destination in a foreign land. God offers Abraham the promise that He will be blessed and his descendants will be blessings to all nations. So Abraham and Sarah accept God's call and begin a life of faith with nothing but a promise and trust in the God of promises.

Living a life of faith proves to be a struggle for Abraham and Sarah as they attempt to trust God and navigate political uncertainty in Egypt, family bickering with Lot, and war with their neighbors. As they get older their concern for not having an heir grows heavy on the hearts and God comes to them again. This time God promises Abraham again that he will have an heir and that his descendants will outnumber the stars in the sky. In the end God blesses them with Isaac and shows himself faithful to Abraham and Sarah as they struggled to be faithful to God.

Jesus fulfills God's promise of blessing to Abraham. Jesus blesses both Jew and Gentile throughout His life. By living a life of faithfulness to God, Jesus shows everyone what it means to have faith in the God of promises. As you continue to prepare for the celebration of Christ's birth and second coming, praise God for the blessing that Jesus has shown you how to live a life of faith.

FOR CHILDREN

A long time after Noah, there was a man called Abraham. God came to him and said, "Pack up your stuff and go on a long trip to a new country."

God promised Abraham, "One day you will have many children and grandchildren in your family. I'll give you a place to call home and you'll care for everyone like I care for you."

The only problem was that both Abraham and his wife Sarah were very old. They were too old to have children. But they trusted God's promise and set out with their family and animals as God asked.

After traveling for a long time, he finally arrived in the country God wanted him to go to. It was a beautiful country and Abraham had to live there as a visitor.

One day some strangers visited Abraham. They had a message from God. "You are going to have a son," they promised.

And Sarah had a baby boy. She named him Isaac.

• What is a promise?

• I wonder how Abraham felt when God made him a promise.

• How would you feel if God made you a promise?

PRAYER

God of Abraham, Isaac, and Jacob, may our life of faith be pleasing to you as we prepare for the coming of your Son from heaven. Amen.

THURSDAY ✦

DAILY PSALM

I love you, LORD, my strength. The LORD is my rock, my fortress and my deliverer; my God is my rock, in whom I take refuge, my shield and the horn of my salvation, my stronghold. (Psalm 18:1-2)

FAMILY DEVOTIONAL • Hang the Jesse Tree Ornament – Genesis 22:1-14

PROMISE PROVIDED

In a terrifying scene to many modern readers, Abraham takes his son Isaac to be killed in obedience to God. The question "why" comes quickly to our minds, along with feelings of doubt about what kind of good God would ask such a thing. The story doesn't focus on God's request, but rather on how Abraham responds to God's request. In other words, the story wants us to ask the question why Abraham would follow through on God's request.

Abraham answers the central question of the story in his reply to Isaac. He says, "God himself will provide." Abraham acts in faith because he knows that God is faithful. He acts in faith that God will keep His promise to bless and protect His people. So Abraham acts on faith.

Faith is easy when life is easy. But when life becomes hard and we need health, financial help, or hope, we may receive nothing beyond the promise that God cares. It is in those moments that living a life of faith becomes a struggle.

Jesus is God's promised sacrifice that provides for our freedom. In Jesus' life, death and resurrection we are reconciled to God, offered forgiveness of sins and invited to live a life of faith. Our preparation during Advent is an act of faith, believing that just as Jesus came to be a living sacrifice we can do the same as we wait in anticipation for His return.

FOR CHILDREN

Isaac was a good son. He helped his father, Abraham, and cared for his family's animals.

One day Abraham took him on trip to a mountain in order to worship God. They didn't take an animal for worship. So Isaac asked Abraham, "Where is the animal for the sacrifice?"

Abraham replied, "God will provide an animal for the sacrifice." And God did provide a sacrifice and saved Isaac's life.

• What do you think a sacrifice is?

• I wonder what things you can thank God for giving you.

• I wonder how Isaac felt when God saved him.

PRAYER

May your promises strengthen us on our Advent journey. Amen.

FRIDAY ✦ Anticipate the Promise

DAILY PSALM

LORD, you alone are my portion and my cup; you make my lot secure. The boundary lines have fallen for me in pleasant places; surely I have a delightful inheritance. I will praise the LORD, who counsels me; even at night my heart instructs me. I keep my eyes always on the LORD. With him at my right hand, I will not be shaken. (Psalm 16:5-8)

FAMILY DEVOTIONAL • Hang the Jesse Tree Ornament – Genesis 28:10-22

PROMISE AFFIRMED

It is often shocking to think of the people God has chosen to use in His work of redeeming the world. Jacob, the heal grasper, the swindler, the con man, and the coward would have to be on the list of shocking people. Jacob, the son of Isaac, tricks his brother out of his birthright and blessing. Then he runs off to his uncle's home. On the way God encounters him in a dream and affirms the promise of Abraham and Isaac with Jacob.

What is it that God saw in Jacob? Why did God choose to affirm the promise with him? Why didn't God choose a more honorable or righteous person?

In Jacob, we encounter the scandal of God's way of redemption. God often chooses the weak, the outcast, and the rough-around-the edges because God does not choose people based on their character. God chooses people based on His freedom to love whomever He will. God teaches us that His love will not be contained to a select group who meet His requirement for love. God's promises are affirmed to folks like Jacob because God will use anyone who responds to His call to participate in His work of redemption.

What great news for everyone this Advent season! The God of Jacob is the same God of Jesus Christ who was sent to save the world and not condemn it. God, out of His freedom to love, has chosen to call everyone to Him. The swindler, the con man, the gangster, the rich, the righteous, and the holy are called by God in order to participate in His work of redemption. The only question is who will respond to God's invitation this Advent in order prepare for the coming Christ.

31

FOR CHILDREN

Isaac married a woman named Rebekah and they had twin sons. The first son was named Esau and he was very hairy. The second was named Jacob and he wasn't hairy.

Isaac wanted to give Esau his special blessing. But Rebekah wanted Jacob to have it. So one day, when Esau was away hunting, Rebekah put animal hair on Jacob's arms.

By now Isaac was very old and blind. Jacob's arms felt hairy, so Isaac thought he was Esau. And Isaac gave Jacob his special blessing!

When Esau found out, he was very angry. "Jacob has stolen my blessing!" he shouted.

Jacob was scared and ran away to his uncle's home.

One night Jacob lay down to sleep. He had a wonderful dream. He saw a stairway to heaven, with angels walking up and down. God spoke to him and said, "The special promise that I gave to your grandfather, Abraham, and your father, Isaac, I am also giving to you. I will give you children, a home, and I will care for you."

• When Jacob woke up next morning, he said, "God is here!"

• What does it mean to steal?

• I wonder how Esau felt when Jacob stole his blessing.

• I wonder how Jacob felt when God gave him a special promise.

PRAYER

Lord of all, may you change our perspective of who you love in order that we may love them and invite them to join us in preparing for the advent of your Son. Amen.

SATURDAY ✦ Anticipate the Promise

DAILY PSALM
Now this I know: The LORD gives victory to his anointed. He answers him from his heavenly sanctuary with the victorious power of his right hand. Some trust in chariots and some in horses, but we trust in the name of the LORD our God. (Psalm 20:6-7)

FAMILY DEVOTIONAL • Hang the Jesse Tree Ornament – Genesis 37:1-11

PROMISE OF PROVIDENCE
God's promise to Abraham, Isaac, and Jacob is always in danger of not being fulfilled. With the presence of evil and death in the world, the people of promise could have been killed or completely turned away from God. But with every new generation, God has been faithful to His promise and provided care, protection and guidance for His people of promise.

Joseph first encountered God's promised providence in a dream. God revealed to Joseph that He was going to use him to lead his whole family in order for God to care for them.

Immediately Joseph began to experience suffering. He is almost killed by his brothers, but instead sold into slavery. He is falsely accused of crimes and thrown into prison. He is promised help when he cares for his fellow inmates, but then is forgotten. Finally God fulfills His promised provision and Joseph becomes a leader in Egypt, preparing them for a great famine. In the end, God reconnects Joseph and his family in Egypt where they bow before Joseph's leadership and God provides food for their family through Joseph.

The first Advent revealed that God's promise of providence comes through suffering. Jesus suffered in order to provide redemption and reconciliation for the world. In preparing for the return of Jesus, we will also experience suffering like Joseph and Jesus as God uses us to provide reconciliation to others. May we all learn this Advent season that suffering is not something to be avoided by Christians, but something to be embraced as the way of God's promised providence.

FOR CHILDREN

Jacob had a big family. He had twelve sons. Jacob loved Joseph more than his other sons. One day Joseph told his brother's about a dream he had. He said, "I dreamt we were in the fields at harvest time. Your bundles of grain bowed down to mine."

Joseph's brothers were very mad. They said, "So you think we should bow down to you?"

The brothers threw him down a dry well. Then they sold him to traders who were going to a far away country. But they told their father Jacob, "Joseph has been killed by a wild animal."

God cared for Joseph through scary times. Eventually, Joseph became a leader in a far away country called Egypt. His brothers came to him because they needed food. Joseph forgave them for the bad things they had done to him. He gave them food to eat. His family moved to Egypt so they had enough to eat.

- I wonder how Joseph felt when his brothers were mean to him.

- I wonder how Joseph felt when he helped his brothers by giving them food.

- How do you feel when someone is mean to you? Do you want to help them?

PRAYER

Come, Lord Jesus and redeem your people from this present evil age that we may celebrate and glorify you in unending fellowship. Amen.

Prepare the Way
A devotional reflection based on Malachi 3:1-4

WARNING

The Advent season is troublesome. The dual focus of Advent on preparing for the celebration of the birth of Christ and the second coming is hard for people to keep in front of them. At times the enthusiasm and excitement for Christmas can eclipse the message of preparation for the return of the Lord. We begin to perceive Advent as merely a time to count down the days to Christmas. On the other extreme, we can focus on our own spiritual condition in preparation for the Lord's appearing and ignore the joy of the good news of Christmas' coming. How can we keep these two extremes in tension and experience Advent as the time of preparation it is?

Our Advent scripture today presents the answer in an odd way. It focuses on preparation, with specific reference to both God's part and our part in preparing to meet and experience God. In other words, Malachi the prophet tells us what needs to be done before the Lord comes. Malachi envisioned the Lord, the true King of Israel, coming suddenly to His people, but not completely without warning. The Lord would send a messenger to prepare the people (v. 1) for their purification (v. 3) and judgment (v. 5).

MESSAGE OF PURIFICATION

The prophet Malachi ministered sometime after the Jewish people had returned from exile to Jerusalem, perhaps around 430 B.C. Despite various reform and restoration projects under Ezra and Nehemiah, the people fell into several spiritual lapses. Malachi called for repentance as a form of preparation and purification of past and present sin.

Purification would be necessary because God wants His people to be righteous as they worship and serve Him (v. 2). Malachi used two images to portray the process of purification. The first reflects the household task of cleaning laundry. The laundry soap Malachi referred to is alkali, a strong bleaching agent used to rid white clothes of stains. The second image comes from the process metalworkers use to separate impurities from the actual gold and silver. Once the Lord has purified His covenant people, they will be fit for fulfilling their purpose and mission in God's kingdom.

PREPARING FOR PURIFICATION

The warning of our purification and judgment helps us, God's people, keep Advent in focus. The first Advent, Christmas, was a time of purification and judgment for the Jewish people. God's people didn't receive their Messiah with the fanfare that was expected. It was a day of joy for a small remnant of Israel's faithful like the shepherds, Mary, and Joseph. It was an unnoticed event for many. But for others, like Herod, it was a time of fear for they rejected God's Christ—the Chosen One. In the same way the return of Christ will be a time for Christians to be purified and judged.

How do we allow the refiner's fire to burn away our impurities and prepare us during this season of Advent? Malachi's message of repentance and trust in God's way is the answer we are given. Repent, or turning toward another way of life, is what we do when we recognize that how we've been living does not line up with God's will for us. In Advent, that means that some of us will need to turn away from our overemphasis on Christmas. For others, it means that we will need to turn away from self-centered spirituality and recognize that there is good news for all in preparing for the coming of Jesus Christ. All of us must turn to God's way, which is to hold in tension of the joy and judgment that the day of Lord is for all and to share that message in word and deed for all.

SUNDAY ✦

DAILY PSALM

Praise the LORD! Sing to the LORD a new song, his praise in the assembly of his faithful people. Let Israel rejoice in their Maker; let the people of Zion be glad in their King. (Psalm 149:1-2)

FAMILY DEVOTIONAL • Hang the Jesse Tree Ornament – Genesis 49:8-12

FAMILY OF KINGS

Jacob reaches the end of his life and calls all of his and Joseph's sons to him in order to bless them. His words are descriptions of their families' roles within the larger family of Israel. Judah's family is described like a lion whose strength is a symbol of their leadership within the animal kingdom. Judah's family is further described as the royal family who will endure until the time "the One" comes.

The Messiah, the Chosen One, is the One who will come from Judah's family and receive the royal staff that is rightfully His. The rightful King of God's people will appear and also be recognized as the King of all nations. People from all around the world will give their allegiance to the Messiah.

Jesus is born into the family of Judah and is the Chosen One spoken of in Judah's blessing. The wise men from foreign nations came to Jesus at His birth and honored Him as King of the Jews, and so Jesus was truly recognized as the King of all nations. And Jesus rode the colt of a donkey in His royal parade into Jerusalem in fulfillment of this blessing given to Judah.

How exciting it is that Jesus is the King of the nations! He has come as the Scriptures foretold, and we can prepare knowing that His second coming will fulfill His role as Lord of all.

FOR CHILDREN

Several years have passed since Joseph's family moved to Egypt. Jacob became sick, and before he died he gathered his twelve sons together. He gave each one a special blessing. He told one of his sons, Judah, that his family would lead the rest of his brother's families like a king.

A long time after Judah was given that special blessing, Jesus was born. Jesus is from Judah's family and is the King of everyone.

• I wonder how it feels to have your parent say something nice to you.

• I wonder how Judah felt when Jacob told him those nice things.

PRAYER

Lord Almighty who reigns forever, may we honor you every day as King as we faithfully serve you. Amen.

MONDAY ✦ Anticipate the King

DAILY PSALM

In you, LORD my God, I put my trust. I trust in you; do not let me be put to shame, nor let my enemies triumph over me. No one who hopes in you will ever be put to shame, but shame will come on those who are treacherous without cause. (Psalm 25:1-3)

FAMILY DEVOTIONAL • Hang the Jesse Tree Ornament – Exodus 14

GOD IS KING

If anything can be observed from the Israelites crossing of the Red Sea it is that God was in control of the whole situation. God was orchestrating where the Israelites went. God was leading the Egyptians to that place. God parted the sea. God defeated the Egyptians. God was in control.

The dramatic story leads to the question, "What kind of God is this?" The answer for the Egyptians is "the God of Israel, who is in control of all creation." To the Israelites the answer is that "God is the LORD Almighty who is their mighty king, strong to deliver. God is the LORD who reigns forever."

Though we live in uncertain days where economic conditions are fragile, political systems are volatile and the future is often feared, we wait in Advent with the realization that our God is the Lord who reigns forever. It is a response of faith to engage each day with the strong assurance that Jesus Christ is the mighty king coming to deliver the world.

FOR CHILDREN

Many years later, after Jacob, Joseph, and his brothers had died, a new Pharaoh or king ruled Egypt. He was mean and hurt Joseph's family. Joseph's family were called Israelites, and they cried to God for help.

One day God sent an angel to an Israelite named Moses. Moses saw a bush that burned brightly but didn't burn up. An angel spoke to Moses from the bush. "God says, 'Return to Egypt. Tell Pharaoh to let my people go so they can worship me!'" So Moses and his brother Aaron went to Egypt. They told Pharaoh, "God says, let my people go!"

But Pharaoh said, "I don't know your God. And I won't let your people go."

So God made terrible things happen in Egypt. Finally, Pharaoh said, "Go!"

So Moses led the Israelites out of Egypt. By day, a pillar of cloud went in front of them. And at night, a pillar made of fire led them. Then Pharaoh changed his mind! He wanted the Israelites back. So he sent his soldiers to chase them.

The Red Sea was in front of the Israelites and the Egyptians were following behind them. The Israelites were trapped! They shook with fear!

God told Moses to hold out his stick—and God parted the water.

All the Israelites marched across on dry ground. But then the waters met again. The Israelites escaped the Egyptian soldiers!

- I wonder how the Israelites felt when Pharaoh sent soldiers to hurt them.
- I wonder how the Israelites felt when God helped them escape.
- What do you think it looked like when the waters of the sea parted?

PRAYER

Lord Almighty who reigns forever, deliver us from evil and lead us in the paths of righteousness for the glory of your name. Amen.

TUESDAY ✦ Anticipate the King

DAILY PSALM

Test me, LORD, and try me, examine my heart and my mind; for I have always been mindful of your unfailing love and have lived in reliance on your faithfulness. (Psalm 26:2-3)

FAMILY DEVOTIONAL • Hang the Jesse Tree Ornament – Exodus 20

TEN COMMANDMENTS OF THE KING

The giving of the Ten Commandments would have been familiar to the Israelites and the ancient readers of Exodus. The story is told in the same manner as a king giving the laws to the people and requiring faithfulness.

The scene opens with God's messenger, Moses, speaking to the people. Moses depicts God as the King who has earned loyalty of the people by delivering them from Egypt. He lists the laws that God has declared to be the boundaries for covenant faithfulness. The Israelites, citizens of God's kingdom, ratify their covenant loyalty by offering a sacrifice to God their king.

In the gospel of Matthew, Jesus begins His ministry by announcing the good news of the kingdom of God coming. In the next scene Jesus is standing on a mountain declaring the rules, or way of life, in God's kingdom. It is clear that Matthew wants us to make the link between the first time God established His kingdom among the Israelites and the second time God ushered His kingdom into the world with Jesus and His followers.

Our preparation is not merely a passive waiting during Advent. We are called to participate in the kingdom of God by obeying the law Jesus lived and taught us. We are to recognize that our true citizenship and loyalty is first and foremost to our God, King Jesus.

FOR CHILDREN

Moses climbed a great mountain called Sinai. At the top he met with God. But Moses was away so long the Israelites thought he was dead. So they made a calf from gold and bowed down to it.

Finally, Moses came down the mountain. He carried two stones with God's good rules on them, called the Ten Commandments. When Moses saw the Israelites praying to a golden calf instead of God, he was furious because they were not obeying God's rules.

• I wonder what Moses said when he talked with God.

• What do you talk to God about?

• I wonder how the Israelites felt when Moses was mad at them for breaking God's rules.

PRAYER

King Jesus come and reign in my heart today. May your laws be a delight to me. Amen.

WEDNESDAY ✦ Anticipate the King

DAILY PSALM

LORD, do not forsake me; do not be far from me, my God. Come quickly to help me, my Lord and my Savior. (Psalm 38:21-22)

FAMILY DEVOTIONAL • Hang the Jesse Tree Ornament – Joshua 6

THE KING GIVES THEM THE LAND

Imagine what it was like to be the Israelites who were getting ready to enter the Promised Land. The land would have been talked about in the stories at their meal times. It would have been the stuff of songs and poems that they would sing during their celebrations. To enter the Promised Land and to live there in peace with God and their neighbors was their deepest desire.

It would have been a crushing blow to hear the report come back from the spies about Jericho. A city that seemed unable to be defeated, yet stood in the way of their promised inheritance.

It seems like "Jerichos" get in the way of our deepest desires during the Advent season. We want to badly to set aside time for family but the work seems overwhelming. We yearn to slow down and spend time with the Lord, but responsibilities pound at our front door and drive us out at an unhealthy pace. We long for giving more to those who are in need but have fewer resources than ever before. Our "Jerichos" can feel like they are unable to be defeated.

The God who fought for Joshua and the Israelites still reigns. As we prepare for Jesus, the wall crusher and Jericho defeater, we can move out in faith by asking for help, saying no to some commitments, and praying that God will make a way for us to experience Advent as the season of preparation He wants it to be. Let us cling to God as our King and trust that He will lead us into the "promised land."

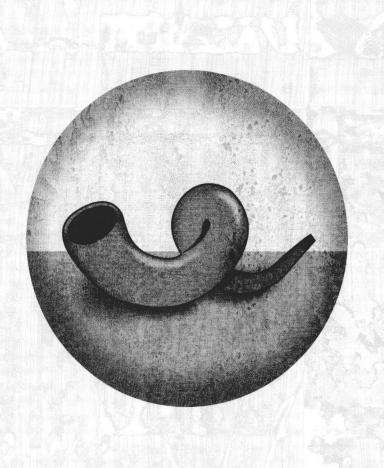

FOR CHILDREN

Joshua was God's chosen leader for the Israelites after Moses died. Joshua led them to the land God promised Abraham, Isaac, Joseph and Joseph's family, the Israelites. They called it the Promised Land.

They marched to the great city of Jericho. God told Joshua what to do in order to capture the city. The Israelites did what God told them to do and marched around the city for six days. But on the seventh day they marched around the city seven times. Then they blew their trumpets and shouted. The walls just tumbled down! And the Israelites moved into the Promised Land that God had given to them.

• I wonder what the city of Jericho looked like.

• Why did Joshua and the Israelites do what God asked them to do?

• I wonder what the trumpets sounded like.

PRAYER

God our provider give us the rest we need, the family bonding we long for, and the means to care for those in need. For your name and glory we ask it. Amen.

THURSDAY ✦ Anticipate the King

DAILY PSALM

Refrain from anger and turn from wrath; do not fret—it leads only to evil. For those who are evil will be destroyed, but those who hope in the LORD will inherit the land. (Psalm 37:8-9)

FAMILY DEVOTIONAL • Hang the Jesse Tree Ornament – Ruth 4

THE KINSMAN REDEEMER

Ruth and Naomi lived in a time when being a widow meant that you were poor. The men in their day owned property and could participate in their agricultural commerce system, the judicial system, and religious system. The women, for the most part, cared for domestic things like clothes, food and household items. So to be without a man who could advocate for you in the greater society meant that you would be unable to care for yourself.

Ruth's commitment to Naomi is dramatic in light of their situation. She stays with Naomi knowing that it would be easier for her to find a husband back in her home country. Yet her love for Naomi keeps her connected to her and ultimately connects Ruth to God.

God provides Ruth and Naomi care and provision through Boaz. Boaz willingly takes the role of kinsman redeemer. That is, he is the one who asked for the right to care for both Ruth and Naomi.

In the same way, Jesus is our kinsman redeemer. We are poor and lost in our sins and brokenness. We have no way of participating in God's way of life. Yet Jesus willingly became our kinsman redeemer in order to care for us and provide a way for us to be reconnected to God.

FOR CHILDREN

Ruth and her mother-in-law Naomi lived far from the Promised Land. Their husbands had died, so Naomi decided to go back to the Promised Land. Ruth went too because she wanted to take care of Naomi.

One day Ruth went to the fields to find food for them to eat. In the fields she met a man called Boaz who was from the family of Judah. He loved Ruth, and they got married. He took care of both Ruth and Naomi. Boaz and Ruth had a son whose name was Obed.

• I wonder how Ruth felt when she met Boaz.

• I wonder what Ruth and Naomi talked about on the way to the Promised Land.

PRAYER

Lord Almighty who reigns forever, we honor you as our redeemer. Amen.

FRIDAY ✦

DAILY PSALM
Love the LORD, all his faithful people! The LORD preserves those who are true to him, but the proud he pays back in full. Be strong and take heart, all you who hope in the LORD. (Psalm 31:23-24)

FAMILY DEVOTIONAL • Hang the Jesse Tree Ornament – 1 Samuel 3:1-21 & 8

A KING IS CHOSEN
Samuel is the first prophet of Israel. He is called by God at a young age and he comes at a time when the faithfulness of the people is diminishing. They are living in the Promised Land, but they keep looking around at all the other nations with kings. They begin to believe that the other nations were more secure with a king then they were. Out of fear that Samuel's sons were not following his ways, the people asked Samuel to appoint a king.

God's reply to Samuel concerning the request of the people is tragic. God said, "Listen to all that the people are saying to you; it is not you they have rejected, but they have rejected me as their king." God tells Samuel that this is nothing new for the Israelites. God says they have been chasing other gods from the day they were rescued from Egypt.

The fear the Israelites have and their lack of faithfulness to God is tragic but not unfamiliar. In Jesus' day His disciples abandoned him at His hour of need. In our day, we forsake God when we run after financial security at the sacrifice of the poor. We say we worship God, but it looks at times we are really worshiping a contemporary style we dress up as God.

Samuel's story serves as a warning to us today. In our fear we can all too often reject God as king. Advent is a time when we can evaluate the kings in our life. The hope is that we will reject all false kings and pledge our allegiance to God and anticipate the celebration of His coming as Lord.

FOR CHILDREN

There was a young boy named Samuel. Samuel's mother brought him to the temple of God. The young boy was going to help Eli the priest.

One night in bed Samuel heard a voice call, "Samuel, Samuel!"

Samuel ran to Eli, "Why did you call me?" he asked.

"I didn't call," Eli said. "It must have been God."

Samuel went back to bed and heard the voice again, "Samuel, Samuel!" This time he listened carefully to God and did all God told him to do. Samuel became God's messenger, or prophet, and God used him to pick the Israelites first king, Saul.

• I wonder what God's voice sounds like.

• Do you think Samuel was scared when he heard God's voice at night?

• What do you think being a messenger means?

PRAYER

Search our hearts God. Reveal our hidden fears. Help us to embrace you as Lord of all. Amen.

SATURDAY ✦ Anticipate the King

DAILY PSALM

Sing the praises of the LORD, you his faithful people; praise his holy name. For his anger lasts only a moment, but his favor lasts a lifetime; weeping may stay for the night, but rejoicing comes in the morning.
(Psalm 30:4-5)

FAMILY DEVOTIONAL • Hang the Jesse Tree Ornament – 1 Samuel 16

THE SHEPHERD OF GOD'S PEOPLE

David is an unlikely pick for the king of the Israelites. David is from a tiny country village that is off the beaten path. He is the youngest of his brothers. He is the son of a shepherd and has spent most of his days out in the wilderness chasing off wild animals and carrying lost sheep back to the flock. He wasn't the strongest, smartest, or the greatest at anything from all indication in the story.

The Scriptures teach us that God likes the unlikely pick. God likes picking the unwanted or least likely people. The reason God often times chooses the most unlikely candidate is that "God does not look at the things people look at. People look at the outward appearance, but God looks at the heart."

Jesus fit God's model for a king perfectly. The Scriptures say that His home town of Nazareth was known for not producing anything worthy of notoriety. Yet, Jesus had the heart that God desires all of us to have. He was a humble king and a gentle shepherd who cares for us daily. May we recognize this Advent those who are the humble servants in our churches and encourage them in their witness for the Lord.

FOR CHILDREN

King Saul didn't always follow God's rules. So God sent Samuel to Jesse, the son of Obed, in order to find the person God wanted to be king of the Israelites.

Jesse had eight sons. They were all passed in front of Samuel. One was strong, and Samuel thought God would want a strong king. But God said, "God does not look at the things people look at. People look at the outward appearance, but God looks at the heart."

Finally, God chose David, the youngest son, to be king. David loved God and tried to do everything God wanted him to do as a king.

• I wonder how David felt when God picked him to be king.

• What do you think David did as king?

• What do you think it means that Jesus is our king?

PRAYER

Gentle King lead us in the way of peace that we might be found as servants to the least when you appear. Amen.

On That Day
A devotional reflection based on Zephaniah 3:14-20

CELEBRATION IN THE PRESENT

The prophet Zephaniah ministered during a turbulent time as foreign powers took turns threatening and/or attacking Judah. Assyria was beginning to weaken, but Babylon was on the rise. What's more, Judah was coming out of the spiritual darkness permitted or encouraged by two corrupt kings. Whichever way he looked at it, Zephaniah saw only bad times on the horizon.

Accordingly, the first two chapters of Zephaniah are full of warnings and exhortations to return to God, in hopes of a deliverance from the impending danger. Chapter 3, however, hints at better times to come, assuming that the people have embraced God, repented, and were truly following him. Zephaniah called his people to respond in celebration, to sing, be glad, and rejoice with all their hearts.

The reason for all this celebration is grounded in the memory of what God had done (v. 15) for His people, and in the promise of what God will do (vv. 16-20). These two perspectives on time, past remembrance and future hope, provide the rationale for celebrating God right now in the present. Zephaniah closes chapter 3, and his book, with the phrase, "before your very eyes," as if to say, "You will witness this grace first hand, and it will turn your sadness into praise and dancing." What a great reminder to celebrate the already and the day to come.

ON THAT DAY

Many faithful followers of Christ enter the Advent season with hopes of reaching the lost, serving the poor, and experiencing God in worship and Christian community. Yet we encounter the evil and brokenness that holds the world captive. We can become discouraged in the good work that God has called us to. We can become overwhelmed at all there is to do and all the needs that exist. For you, Zephaniah has an encouraging message for the future. He wants to tell you what that day will be like for the faithful ones of God.

First, for those who are in Christ Jesus, God will remove His judgment from you. He will look at all of the faithful on that day and burst forth in song. Those who are the faithful of the Lord will know how much joy and happiness that you bring to God.

Second, God will gather all of the faithful together. For the Jewish people of Zephaniah's day that meant a return to the Promised Land. For us today that means a gathering of all God's people across all time and distance in the new creation. The gathering will be enormous and reveal the kingdom of God with its small beginnings for the cosmic community God has created it to be. On that day the celebration will be so intense that all mourning will be removed.

Finally, the faithful of the Lord are encouraged to enter into that day right now. With the knowledge of all that God has done in the past and with the joyous hope that is in front of us. We are to enter into the celebration today.

SUNDAY ✦ Anticipate the Prophecy

DAILY PSALM

Sing to the LORD a new song, for he has done marvelous things; his right hand and his holy arm have worked salvation for him. The LORD has made his salvation known and revealed his righteousness to the nations. He has remembered his love and his faithfulness to Israel; all the ends of the earth have seen the salvation of our God. (Psalm 98:1-3)

FAMILY DEVOTIONAL • Hang the Jesse Tree Ornament – 1 Kings 3:3-14

WISDOM

Solomon could be thought of as a king who was an aspiring prophet. The prophet did not just foretell God's future activity. Often the prophet did the task of forthtelling. Foretelling is a prediction, or in the case of God's prophet it was an announcement of God's future activity, that was revealed to them by God. Forthtelling is the announcement of the consequences for what is currently happening. In church, the preacher at times discerns what is happening in society or the church and by the power of the Spirit tells what will come forth from the current situation. Solomon's request for discernment falls into the prophetic work of forthtelling. He desired to know a godly perspective on life and rightly discern a consequence that would glorify God.

This Advent what we need is to prepare in a godly way and so we stand in need of discernment. May God give the gift of the prophet to rightly discern God's activity and a faithful response in our day.

FOR CHILDREN

When David died, his son Solomon became king of Israel. God asked Solomon to build Him a building called a temple where people could come and worship and pray to God. Solomon built a beautiful temple for God. Inside, he put a special box called the ark of the covenant of the Lord. It was to remind Israel of God's presence with them. When the temple was finished, people came from near and far to pray there.

• Do you know where we go to worship God?

• Why do you think Solomon wanted to build God a temple?

• I wonder how God felt when Solomon built Him a temple.

PRAYER

God of wisdom may the light of your Son shine through the darkness this Advent and may your children know your will in these days. Amen.

MONDAY ✦ Anticipate the Prophecy

DAILY PSALM

I am like an olive tree flourishing in the house of God; I trust in God's unfailing love forever and ever. For what you have done I will always praise you in the presence of your faithful people. And I will hope in your name, for your name is good. (Psalm 52:8-9)

FAMILY DEVOTIONAL • Hang the Jesse Tree Ornament – 1 Kings 17:1-16

IDOL WORSHIP

Being a prophet is risky business. Elijah's story reveals the deadly realities of being faithful to God. We catch up with Elijah after he has just told Ahab, king of Israel, that there will be drought because of the idol worship he has allowed. Ahab doesn't accept Elijah's prophecy and begins to plot his capture and death.

Idols are all around us. We give our money to the idol of material goods. We sacrifice our Sundays to the gods of football and/or basketball. We pay tribute to the idol of technology with the hours we spend online or gaming.

Elijah's story encourages us to confront the idol worship in our day. God sustains and cares for Elijah following his courageous act of faith in declaring God's message to Ahab. By delivering food on the wings of ravens and a miraculous provision of flour and oil for a foreigner who cares for Elijah, God teaches us that He sustains His faithful servants.

And the same is true of Jesus' story. Christ confronts all the idols of our world in His death, and God resurrects Him to reveal that faithfulness to God will always overcome the idolatry in our world.

Some of Israel's kings were good, like David. Others were bad. One bad king, named Ahab, told his people not to worship God.

God sent Elijah, one of his messengers, to Ahab. "Tell God you are sorry, or there will be no rain. No crops will grow. Your people will go hungry." But Ahab laughed. He did not tell God he was sorry. So it didn't rain.

Ahab was angry with Elijah and wanted to catch him. So Elijah ran away to the desert. But how would he find food there?

God brought Elijah to a stream where he could drink. And He sent ravens with food to eat.

Later God sent Elijah to a poor woman who lived with her son. "Please give me something to eat," he said.

The woman had only enough flour and oil to make one loaf. But she shared it with Elijah.

"God will give us food," Elijah said. After that there was always enough flour and oil.

• Why was Ahab angry at Elijah?

• I wonder what food the ravens brought to Elijah.

PRAYER

As we prepare for your return, resurrected Lord, may your victory over sin and idolatry spur us on to be faithful to you this Advent season. Amen.

TUESDAY ✦ Anticipate the Prophecy

DAILY PSALM

My heart is stirred by a noble theme as I recite my verses for the king; my tongue is the pen of a skillful writer. You are the most excellent of men and your lips have been anointed with grace, since God has blessed you forever. (Psalm 45:1-2)

FAMILY DEVOTIONAL • Hang the Jesse Tree Ornament – Isaiah 53

PROPHECY OF THE SERVANT

Throughout the story of Israel, we've explored how suffering is a part of being used of God to bless the world. The suffering that Abraham, Sarah, and Joseph encountered as they lived the life of faith prepared us to hear Isaiah's prophecy of God's Messiah suffering.

Yet, Isaiah's prophecy is still shocking. God's Messiah will be despised. He will be the one that people ridicule. He will be the type of person that people will go out of their way to not have to be around. That level of rejection is shocking and one can begin to see why no one expected God's Messiah to really fit Isaiah's prophecy.

Jesus' disciples wouldn't believe that He was to die. Their mindset was that of "death is for the weak who can't stop the powerful from killing them." But Jesus embraced His calling to suffer on our behalf. He took the rejection from the disciples and remained faithful to God.

As we prepare for the second coming of Christ and the celebration of His first coming, are we prepared to embrace His role as suffering servant? Will we follow His way of sacrifice in order to love God and others? This is the way Jesus has laid out for us as His followers. Let's pray that God will give us the courage and grace to follow.

FOR CHILDREN

Israel didn't do what God asked them to do so bad things began to happen to them.

God sent Isaiah, one of His messengers, to the Israelites. Isaiah told them that the bad things would not happen to them forever. God was going to send a servant who would rescue them. He said that the servant would be punished in their place.

• Why did bad things happen to the Israelites?

• How do you feel when bad things happen to you?

PRAYER

God of love lead us into your way of life even if it means that we suffer for your work of redemption in our world. Amen.

WEDNESDAY ✦ Anticipate the Prophecy

DAILY PSALM

You are my portion, LORD; I have promised to obey your words. I have sought your face with all my heart; be gracious to me according to your promise. I have considered my ways and have turned my steps to your statutes. (Psalm 119:57-59)

FAMILY DEVOTIONAL • Hang the Jesse Tree Ornament – Jeremiah 31:31-34

PROPHECY OF A NEW COVENANT

Jeremiah began his ministry as a prophet during the reign of Josiah. Josiah was the last righteous king of Judah. After a copy of the Law of Moses was found in the temple, Josiah attempted to enact reforms in order to rid Judah of idol worship. Josiah succeeded in removing the outward structures and practices of idolatry. Yet the hearts of the people were not changed.

This prophecy of Jeremiah comes years after Josiah's death. The people have experienced a succession of four evil kings. All hope for a renewal of covenant faithfulness among God's people seems small.

Against this context the prophecy of a new covenant written on the hearts of people would be a source of great hope for the faithful few. The new covenant will be like the original covenant. Except this time God is going to get to the core issue. The people of His new covenant need their hearts transformed. Instead of a heart that is continually inclined toward evil, God will make a way for their hearts to be fixed on God's law or covenant way of life.

We can celebrate that God has done this in Jesus. As we prepare to praise God for the gift of His son, we can also praise Him for the new covenant He has poured out to all those who are in Christ Jesus. We don't need to merely make outward changes this Advent. In Christ, we can experience a transformation of the heart.

FOR CHILDREN

The Israelites had more bad kings, like Ahab, who led the Israelites to not obey God. God sent Jeremiah, one of His messengers, to tell the Israelites to obey God. Jeremiah was sad because they didn't listen to him.

One day God told him that things won't always stay this way. God said, "There will be a day when I make a new promise with Israel and they will love what I ask them to do."

• Why do you think the Israelites didn't obey God?

• What is a promise?

PRAYER

God the Father let your Spirit move within us and transform us from the inside out through the new covenant in Christ. Amen.

THURSDAY ✦

DAILY PSALM

I waited patiently for the LORD; he turned to me and heard my cry. He lifted me out of the slimy pit, out of the mud and mire; he set my feet on a rock and gave me a firm place to stand. He put a new song in my mouth, a hymn of praise to our God. Many will see and fear the LORD and put their trust in him. (Psalm 40:1-3)

FAMILY DEVOTIONAL • Hang the Jesse Tree Ornament – Habakkuk 3:16-19

FAITHFUL WAITING

The book of Habakkuk begins with a question. Basically the question is, "God, why is there evil?" More specifically Habakkuk wants to know why God has not acted to stop the evil in the world. He is a prophet just before Judah will be taken into exile by Babylon. He's known evil and seen the injustices caused by God's people and other nations his whole life. So his prophecy begins with the question, "Why?"

God is patient and listens to him. Then God replies and says that He is going to send the Babylonians to punish the people of God.

Habakkuk asks the question again, but this time pointed at why God would allow the Babylonians to go unpunished. Habakkuk finishes this interrogation of God with the image of waiting. He says he will be stationed on a watchtower and keeping a lookout for God.

God is patient and listens to him. Then God tells Habakkuk that He is in control. In essence, God will do what God will do and that should be enough.

Habakkuk prays in response to God. The prayer is a confession of Habakkuk's need of God and God's greatness. In short, Habakkuk agrees with God's reply. No matter what happens, whether we like the outcome or not, God is still God and is in control of His creation.

FOR CHILDREN

Habakkuk was a messenger sent from God to one part of God's people called Judah. Judah did not obey God.

There was a bad country called Babylon. They were going to hurt the people of Judah. Habakkuk asked God on behalf of the people why all these bad things were going to happen. God said, "Trust me and obey me because I am in control."

• How do you obey your parents?

• How do you obey God?

PRAYER

Though the fig tree does not bud and there are no grapes on the vines, though the olive crop fails and the fields produce no food, though there are no sheep in the pen and no cattle in the stalls, yet I will rejoice in the LORD, I will be joyful in God my Savior. (Habakkuk 3:16-19)

FRIDAY ✦ Anticipate the Prophecy

DAILY PSALM

The Mighty One, God, the LORD, speaks and summons the earth from the rising of the sun to where it sets. From Zion, perfect in beauty, God shines forth. Our God comes and will not be silent; a fire devours before him, and around him a tempest rages. He summons the heavens above, and the earth, that he may judge his people: "Gather to me this consecrated people, who made a covenant with me by sacrifice." And the heavens proclaim his righteousness, for he is a God of justice.
(Psalm 50:1-6)

FAMILY DEVOTIONAL • Hang the Jesse Tree Ornament – Nehemiah 6:15-16; 8; 9

THE RETURN

After years of exile, God is gathering His people back in the Promise Land. Under the leadership of Nehemiah the walls of Jerusalem are rebuilt. Despite the opposition and plots to sabotage the construction, the people are able to accomplish the construction project because God has been helping them.

Following the completion of the wall, Ezra and Nehemiah lead the people in renewing their covenant with God. There is a reading of the Law, a celebration for God's great work in their midst, and then finally they confess the sins of the whole Israelite community from beginning to their day and pledge to follow God.

What is apparent from these texts is that God's faithfulness is what sustains our relationship. In other words, it is God's grace that allows for a second, a third, a fourth, and who knows how many more chances. God is patient with humans, and He continually chooses to come after us.

We can celebrate this Advent season that God has provided a second chance for everyone in the sending of His Son. For He sent the Son into the world not to condemn the world, but to save it (John 3:17).

FOR CHILDREN

God's people, Israel and Judah, were hurt by other countries and taken away from the Promised Land. Years later God started bringing His people back to the Promised Land, but they found the walls of Jerusalem, God's special city, were broken.

God chose Nehemiah to lead the people in rebuilding the walls. Nehemiah asked the king he served if he could rebuild the walls. The king said yes and gave him supplies to help because God was with Nehemiah.

Many people tried to stop Nehemiah and God's people from rebuilding the walls. But they finished rebuilding the walls of Jerusalem with God's help.

• Have you ever been chosen to do something special?

• How did you feel when you were chosen?

• I wonder how Nehemiah felt when God chose him to rebuild the walls.

PRAYER

God of second chances renew our faith today that we might be a means of grace to our neighbor this day. Amen.

SATURDAY ✦ Anticipate the Prophecy

DAILY PSALM
Cast your cares on the LORD and he will sustain you; he will never let the righteous be shaken. (Psalm 55:22)

FAMILY DEVOTIONAL • Hang the Jesse Tree Ornament – Luke 1:57-80

ANTICIPATION
Zechariah had to wait 9 months before he could tell anyone the details of his encounter with the angel Gabriel. He had to wait 9 months to articulate his shock. He had to wait 9 months to praise God in song. He had to wait 9 months to tell Elizabeth how blessed her joy made him. Zechariah is the picture of anticipation for us. He knows the great and wonderful thing that is coming, but he must wait before he can tell others the whole story. His one and only son will be coming into the world, and he knows God has chosen him to prepare the way for God's Messiah. Yet he wouldn't be able to share that with someone in an intimate conversation.

And when that day came, Zechariah burst forth into praise. He praised God for His covenant faithfulness to Israel. He praised God for His Son and the role He would get to play in redemption history. He praised God for fulfilling the prophecies and for the Messiah being close at hand.

The long awaited hope is close. The anticipation is overwhelming. Come Lord, Jesus.

FOR CHILDREN

God's people waited for the servant of God to come and rescue them. They waited for hundreds of years. Finally an angel came to Zechariah, an Israelite who obeyed God. The angel said, "You and your wife, Elizabeth are going to have a child. You are to name him John. He will prepare God's people for the servant of God to come."

Zechariah doubted what the angel told him because he and Elizabeth were old and couldn't have children. So the angel said, "You will be silent and not able to speak until your baby is born, because you did not believe what I told you."

And everything happened just the way God's angel said it would. Zechariah and Elizabeth had a baby boy and named him John.

• I wonder if Zechariah was scared when he saw God's angel.

• What would you do if you couldn't talk?

• How do you think Zechariah told people about the angel if he couldn't talk?

PRAYER

Praise God, from Whom all blessings flow;
Praise Him, all creatures here below;
Praise Him above, ye heavenly host;
Praise Father, Son, and Holy Ghost.[1]

O Little Town of Bethlehem
A devotional reflection based on Micah 5:2-5a

HUMBLE BEGINNINGS
The prophet Micah was a contemporary of Hosea and Isaiah, around 735-700 B.C., several hundred years after King David's reign when the united kingdom had split in two. Micah's message was delivered to both the Northern kingdom of Israel and the Southern kingdom of Judah, stressing the need for justice and peace. He also warned of the impending destruction that would surely fall if they continued to ignore or disregard these core elements of God's will for His people.

Micah preached in the typical prophetic style that reflected the three major movements of a courtroom trial of that day: Attention, Accusation and Verdict, and Promise. Chapters 3-5 follow this pattern with a condemnation of the leaders—priests, judges, and false prophets alike—and a dire warning of what will happen to them and the nation if they do not repent. Chapters 4 and 5 paint a picture of better times after the impending doom.

Part of Micah's vision of the future included a description of a coming king who would restore order and justice in a new kingdom. Then all the suffering would be ended (even though they brought it on themselves by sinning) and justice would prevail.

Micah's model was King David, who had risen from a boy watching his father's sheep on the hills outside the small, insignificant town of Bethlehem to become king. Micah recognized that God tends to choose lowly and unexpected people to do His will (Moses, Israel, Ruth, David, and later, Mary), and he worked this fact into his vision of the coming king (5:2-5). Those who assumed that Israel would be rebuilt on principles of power and prestige would have been surprised by Micah's declaration that the coming king "will be their peace" (v. 5).

O LITTLE TOWN OF BETHLEHEM
Advent is an important time of the year for Christians. The meaning and significance we place on this time lead some to think that we need

to enter into it in huge ways. We plan for big productions of live nativities where we can draw in hundreds of people. We orchestrate extravagant giveaways to new visitors in order to wow them by our generosity. We spend countless hours preparing for gifts, family, dinners, and parties. In the midst of all the extravagant giving and huge productions, the small and seemingly insignificant may be shunned. We rationalize that if we truly are going to celebrate then "bigger is better."

The message of Micah pushes back on the "bigger is better" mentality. If we despise small beginnings and insist on seeing everything before we get on board, we will miss out on joining what God is doing. For Micah points to the backwater village of Bethlehem where one of the greatest kings of Israel emerged and announces that from this insignificant place, God will reveal His immense mercy. In short, the prophet wants us to embrace God's way of working: little rural town, peasant girl, manger, lowly shepherds, and cross. God takes the small, little, and seemingly insignificant and reveals the strength and majesty of His name to the ends of the earth.

The little town of Bethlehem teaches us this Advent season to embrace the way of God. We are taught to embrace our limitations as opportunities to trust the unlimited ability of God. We are taught to revel in small acts of kindness, little conversations over coffee, tiny homemade gifts and simple notes of love as a means of God's enormous grace. As we gaze upon that manger in that little town in the middle of nowhere Israel, we should praise the Creator of all things for coming to us in peace and shepherding us into the celebration of His return.

O holy Child of Bethlehem,
Descend on us, we pray.
Cast out our sin, and enter in;
Be born in us today.
We hear the Christmas angels
The great glad tidings tell.
O come to us; abide with us,
Our Lord Emmanuel.[2]

SUNDAY ✦ Anticipate the Coming

DAILY PSALM

Ascribe to the LORD, you heavenly beings, ascribe to the LORD glory and strength. Ascribe to the LORD the glory due his name; worship the LORD in the splendor of his holiness. (Psalm 29:1-2)

FAMILY DEVOTIONAL • Hang the Jesse Tree Ornament – Luke 1:26-38

HOPE

God's promise to send the Christ is about to happen. As Isaiah wrote, "Therefore the Lord himself will give you a sign: The virgin will conceive and give birth to a son, and will call him Immanuel." (Isaiah 7:14)

The Virgin Mary is our example of hope in the Christmas story. Engaged to be married and being found with child would have meant death at worse, or being labeled an outcast at least. Knowing the consequences ahead of her, Mary still chooses to serve God.

With one of the greatest hope-filled expressions in all of Scripture Mary says to Gabriel, "I am the Lord's servant. May your word to me be fulfilled." Mary doesn't know if what she is choosing with has the best positive outcome. She does know that it makes her future uncertain. Her relationships become complicated. But more important she knows that her choice is to hope in God. She is hoping that God will sustain her and use her for His work of redemption.

You may be struggling with decisions about life. You know the consequences of your options. You know the pros and cons. Yet you are struggling with where your hope lies. Let Mary's choice serve as a guide for you. Put your hope in God by choosing to participate in His mission to redeem the world through Jesus Christ.

FOR CHILDREN

God's angel came to Mary, a young Israelite girl who was engaged to marry Joseph, a descendant of King David. The angel said, "Greetings. The Lord is with you. Do not be afraid. God is pleased with you. You will have a baby boy and you are to call him Jesus. He will be God's servant who will rescue God's people. He will be a great king like David and His kingdom will never end."

"How will this be?" Mary asked the angel.

The angel answered, "God the Holy Spirit will do this and it will not fail."

"I am the Lord's servant," Mary answered. "May everything you say come true." And everything the angel told her happened.

• What do you think it means to be a servant?

• I wonder how Mary felt about her decision to serve the Lord.

PRAYER

View the present through the promise, Christ will come again.
Trust despite the deepening darkness, Christ will come again.
Lift the world above its grieving through your watching and believing
in the hope past hope's conceiving: Christ will come again.[3]

MONDAY ✦ Anticipate the Coming

DAILY PSALM

Truly my soul finds rest in God; my salvation comes from him. Truly he is my rock and my salvation; he is my fortress, I will never be shaken. (Psalm 62:1-2)

FAMILY DEVOTIONAL • Hang the Jesse Tree Ornament – Luke 2:1-20

MANGER

Today in the town of David a Savior has been born to you; he is the Messiah, the Lord. (Luke 2:11)

The day has finally come. All the waiting, prayers, hopes, dreams, struggles, joy and pain is over. We've made it to the manger. We've made it to the fulfillment of God's promises and prophecies. The Savior has been born, and we can all celebrate.

What a foretaste of what it will be like at the second coming for all of those who are in Christ Jesus. Every faithful follower of God will experience the same kind of joy and excitement that Christmas brings to little children with gifts to open. It is such a pure joy that we will not be able to contain our songs of praise or dancing with glee.

"Glory to God in the highest heaven, and on earth peace to those on whom His favor rests." (Luke 2:14)

FOR CHILDREN

Away in a manger
No crib for His bed
The little Lord Jesus
Laid down His sweet head.

The stars in the bright sky
Looked down where He lay
The little Lord Jesus
Asleep on the hay.

The cattle are lowing
The poor Baby wakes
But little Lord Jesus
No crying He makes.

I love Thee, Lord Jesus
Look down from the sky
And stay by my side,
'Til morning is nigh.

Be near me, Lord Jesus,
I ask Thee to stay
Close by me forever
And love me I pray.

Bless all the dear children
In Thy tender care
And take us to heaven
To live with Thee there.[4]

PRAYER

Joy to the world, the Lord is come!
Let earth receive her King;
Let every heart prepare Him room,
And Heaven and nature sing.[5]

TUESDAY ✦ Anticipate the Coming

DAILY PSALM

May the peoples praise you, God; may all the peoples praise you. May the nations be glad and sing for joy, for you rule the peoples with equity and guide the nations of the earth. May the peoples praise you, God; may all the peoples praise you. (Psalm 67:3-5)

FAMILY DEVOTIONAL • Hang the Jesse Tree Ornament – John 1:1-14

THE LORD

The Word became flesh and made his dwelling among us. (John 1:14a)

The Word, the Logos, has entered His creation in human flesh. How comforting it is to know that in a world where everything seems to be disconnected and people seem so distant that our God has chosen to draw near. The Word, who brought forth creation, was born into His creation. He came to participate in His creation in order to show humans how we are supposed to worship God as living sacrifice.

This is reason to celebrate. Gather with family and friends. Sing songs of praise. Dance for the Lord. Celebrate how amazing God—Father, Son and Holy Spirit—is for drawing near to us.

FOR CHILDREN

In the beginning Jesus was with God, and Jesus was God. He was with God in the beginning. Through him everything was created. God sent John as a messenger to prepare people to believe in who Jesus is. And this is what we believe: Jesus is God's one and only Son who was born and lived among people.

• What does "Jesus is God's son" mean?

PRAYER

Then let us all with one accord,
Sing praises to our heavenly Lord.

Appendix: Suggested Family Devotional Practice For Anticipate

SET A TIME
It's important to set a time for family devotionals. The set time will allow children to get into a routine and a rhythm. Try a couple of different times to find what works with your family. Once you find a good time, stick with it through the Advent season.

JESSE TREE ORNAMENTS
You have two options for using the Jesse Tree Ornaments. First, you could cut the symbols out of the book each day and create them into an ornament. The other option is to check out adventexperience.com to download the Jesse Tree symbols and to find craft ideas for creating ornaments with your family.

FOR FAMILIES WITH TEENAGER(S)
• Read the passage

• Read the devotional

• Talk about any thoughts that came from the reading

• Write or talk about prayer requests

• Pray

FOR FAMILIES WITH PRE-SCHOOL CHILDREN
Instead of reading the passage and devotional above you may want to read the children's version of the Bible story.

Notes

1. "Praise God from Whom All Blessing Flow." *Sing to the Lord Hymnal* (Kansas City: Lillenas Publishing Company, 1993), p. 6.

2. "O Little Town of Bethlehem." Ibid, p. 169.

3. "A View of the Past Through the Present." Words by Thomas Troeger, 1986. Ibid, p. 286.

4. "Away in a Manger." Ibid, p. 176

5. "Joy to the World." Ibid, p. 173.